FAIRVIEW

Spirits that walk on the earth are
not always what we think they are.

Sharon Taylor King

Copyright Page

© 2025 Sharon Taylor King
Fairview
First Printing
Book #2

All rights reserved. Reproduction in whole or part without written permission from the publisher or author is strictly prohibited. Printed in the United States of America.

This is non-fiction,
A book inspired by the Holy Spirit,
Who teaches us all things.

All Scripture is taken from several versions of the Holy Bible, public domain.

Sharon Taylor King
Corbin, Kentucky

Kindle Direct Publishing

CONTENTS

Introduction ....Page 4

Chapter 1: Fairview ....Page 6

Chapter 2: It Was Quiet......................Page 14

Chapter 3: My Aunt's Farm ....Page 18

Chapter 4: Battles Will Be Fought.....Page 23

Chapter 5: I Don't Know What Happened at Fairview..Page 30

Chapter 6: My Oil Paintings ....Page 35

Chapter 7: Faith over Fear ....Page 42

Chapter 8: Haunted Houses ....Page 51

Chapter 9: Prayer is a Weapon ....Page 56

Chapter 10: Superstition ....Page 65

Author's Book Shelf ....Page 73

Author's Pictures ....Page 75

INTRODUCTION

In today's society it's popular to chase after spirits. Many believe they're ghosts; human being spirits who have passed and have never really left earth. Little do they realize but what they are really chasing after are demons. These demons are dangerous to human beings because they seek to possess and take souls to hell.

Some of these demons have been in a human and when he or she passed on, they're turned loose seeking another body to possess. They take control sometimes by using fear to control a person. This is spiritual warfare and can only be fought in the spiritual realm. The God we serve has power over the enemy, but we must turn to Him and pray for help.

There are satanic people who also open doors for demons to enter. They are worshippers of the devil, many times leave places that are full of evil.

This book tells of the experiences my family and I had in a house that was full of demons. It was a doorway where evil came in and out. It caused us to live in anxiety and fear constantly. This was not a fun time as some may believe that dealing with these things are. It was a trial of our faith.

FAIRVIEW

CHAPTER ONE

As I look at the painting on the wall of the old house standing so stately and warm, I'm reminded of so many memories surrounding the old place of both good and bad.

We lived at the time in a small house with two bedrooms. So when dad found this large house with three floors and a basement we were delighted. It was a beautiful house.

There was my mom, dad, brother and myself. The main floor of the house had a large hallway and stairs going to the upstairs and an arched doorway to the living room, which led to the dining room and then the kitchen. The kitchen had a doorway to the basement which had four rooms. One was just storage; one was the laundry room and one was where a large round furnace was, which had been converted from a coal furnace to a gas one. The last room down there was an old coal room with a shoot where coal was put in from outside. The stairway in the hallway at the entrance led to the bedrooms. My bedroom was in the middle of the upstairs hall at the top of the stairs; my brother's was to the right and mom and dad's was to the left of me. I had French windows.

The floors were all hardwoods; they were very beautiful except for a a few very large stains on the main floor level. The attic was on the third level of the house and it became our family room. It had a full bath and a half off of the bedrooms.

It all began the year we bought the old place. It was referred to as *'Jones old haunted house.'* The former owners of the house were the Jones. I was fourteen at the time. I had just started junior high school nearby. Students at the school started to tease my brother and I as soon as they found out where we lived. My brother was eighteen months older than me and he would tell me scary stories he had heard from the students at school.

I'd met my boyfriend a few months prior at church. He was a preacher. He was only fifteen years old but saved and preached the gospel. This really impressed me. Our house was considered uptown from where he lived. He lived you might say across the tracks. He was a young man with a very level head; a large boy for his age, when he became a man, he was 6'4" tall and a big boned man.

Mom and dad played music and sang in church. They both were ministers. I sang with my parents and played the piano. This young teenaged minister held a revival, and I went to hear him preach of course. I bragged on his sermon and because at the time, he was a young minister who caught the eyes of most girls in the church including myself. He came to visit us in our house a few times before we moved into our new place and then came on a regular basis after we moved in.

The house was friendly and warm and welcomed us in as old friends. The sun would shine through the windows so bright and the house seemed so free from evil and the light permeated the old house. But oh the secrets that old house did hold were revealed in years to come. Fairview as I refer to it now was just the street name then, now it holds the name of the painting. Behind its innocent exterior holds secrets and memories that time can never erase. During the first year or so things there were quiet although at times there were strange noises which we explained away. It seems as I recall it all began on New Year's Eve and we had a prayer meeting there. Only God knows for sure, but from then on things just really got out of hand.

There were spaces of quiet but we heard people talking and we saw odd things. You could never or very seldom understand what they were saying unless it was one of our names spoken. Whatever it was, it would imitate our voices to each other and we also heard laughing and crying.

There were two bathrooms, a full bath and a half, from the upstairs hallway. One day I was in the full bathroom and my mother was on the phone in the hall, and she heard me crying but I wasn't crying. I was at the end of the hallway and heard nothing. One morning I was still asleep and it was Saturday and my mother heard me call her from downstairs. She happened to look in my bedroom and saw me sleeping; a voice just like mine was coming from downstairs.

My dad got up early one morning and started into the kitchen to put the coffee on when he saw someone fading out while sitting at the kitchen table.

This had been one spree but things went quiet again but then one evening we all were watching TV upstairs in the attic and I decided to go downstairs and wash the dishes. We had swinging café doors going into the kitchen. Dad put them up for decoration. I started to wash the dishes at the sink when I heard the doors move. I looked at them but saw nothing. I thought I had just imagined it but then I heard something in the dining area. I began to get frightened, so I thought I'd check it out to reassure myself, so I would no longer be afraid. So I went to the doors to see. I looked over the doors and there was a round chair sitting in the doorway from the living room to the dining room. As I looked a woman with long dark hair was sitting in the chair leaning back smiling at me. I began to scream and didn't even know how I got back up the stairway, but when the family returned to see with me, she was no longer there anymore. There was nothing.

My boyfriend and I had an argument over some girl and he hadn't been calling me for days, but the night I saw the woman he called about an hour after that happened. My mother answered the phone and he said how was I and if anything strange had happened. I wondered if he had been involved with this in some way somehow. He had been going to different kinds of churches looking at different beliefs. I know he went to a snake-handling church, a prophetic church and he was going at the time to some spiritualism church. Maybe he sent a spirit to visit me and knew they were coming. He never told me but I can't help but feel he must've been involved in some way from his phone call. I'll never know he has passed on now.

We anointed the house with oil and prayed over it. Then we opened the door to usher this evil spirit out of our house once and for all. It had to be removed and extracted from the house. We felt it had left and was gone. The house became quiet and pleasant again for some time.

Mom and dad went out one evening and left myself and brother alone in the house. I was around fifteen at this time; my brother was 18 months older than I was. I can't even remember what it was about but like siblings, we got into an argument. My brother all at once stopped arguing and he went into his room. He told me to go to mine and pray. I was in the hall upstairs and I didn't understand, I was still quarreling.

I said, *"Why would you tell me that you are going to push me down the stairs?"*

But as I was standing there a very strong, powerful spirit started at my head and came all the way down to my feet. I could feel the eerie presence, as it was moving from the head down. It was fearful and undesirable. I began to pray, I went into my room and I knew my brother was praying. It was a feeling like something awful had happened and we knew it. Mom and dad had come home and I let them in and my brother was so deep in prayer, he had not even heard the door.

My brother was to experience several things in the months to come, especially when he was in the house alone. We all were at church one night except for him when he started down the stairs when someone put their hand on his shoulder as if to stop him. He didn't even look around, he just said,

"Hey I am on your side."

And it lifted. I don't guess he cared at the time what side of good or evil they were on just as long as he was alright. He saw monsters one night like bugs or creatures like demons or whatever he saw was not good? The house seemed to turn into an opening for spirits to come and go and I feel for sure, they were demons. We'll probably never know for sure until Judgment Day and it won't matter by then.

IT WAS QUIET

CHAPTER TWO

The quiet came and went, then one night we had funny books downstairs and I decided to go downstairs after bedtime to get them to read before we went to sleep. We got them from the living room then turned the hall light off downstairs going upstairs. My mom was joking and said, what if she comes referring to the woman I saw in the round chair. Just about that time a woman croaking like a witch, if you can imagine would have said something behind us. I was behind mom on the stairs but somehow I managed to leave her, and get around her on the stairs. Next, I knew she came up behind me screaming. Then all of a sudden things became quiet again and we began to play again.

One Thanksgiving my cousins and aunt came for the holidays. My boyfriend was there also. There was a snowstorm and we went out into the yard and had a snowball fight. We then went back inside to get warm by the furnace in our basement. My brother and sometimes my mom and dad would play with us.

My dad preached but he also held down a full-time job as a chemical operator. He worked different shifts and when he left for work we'd form a train-playing from the hallway to the dining area and living room; back to the hallway. My boyfriend would say, as soon as dad left, it started.

We dated other people some and I had had a small framed, good dancing boyfriend up at my house one evening. We were listening to records in the living room. The family was upstairs watching TV and coming in and out of the kitchen, of course checking on us too.
He and I were sitting in the round chair when all at once the window shades sprung open to the tops of the window, scaring both of us. He had heard about this house and he jumped into my lap, so fast I couldn't believe it. I laughed; he was a cousin by marriage to my other boyfriend. So I wasn't really dating either of them after this, and this smaller one was also dating a neighbor girl around the corner from me. My boyfriend was

sitting across the street at a Catholic Church lawn watching my house for a new boyfriend to show up. The one told the other one to help him watch. I had no boyfriend there or coming, so dad and I decided to put on an overcoat on him, and for me to kiss him at the door. Then dad started walking and they started to follow him, thinking he was my boyfriend. Dad began to run, they ran after him and dad ran around the block and back to sit on the porch waiting for them. They ran up on him, and the small one didn't know my dad and he said, *"Well, get him."* But the bigger boy told him, that's her father. They got really mad and went home. They never watched my house again. My brother was ready to run when my dad came back to act like he was the real boyfriend, but they'd had enough. We got a good laugh out of it.

A little cousin of mine, a girl a little younger than me wanted to stay all night in the haunted house and she was sleeping with me until she heard snoring coming from the bed by her head and it wasn't me. She never stayed another night.

One of my aunts came by with her baby girl, and she was around three years of age. She was playing in the dining room and she said someone is talking to me, but I can't see them. My mom went in there fussing, saying, *"You scared a little baby, if you're in here knock once."* It did respond to several knock questions.

One night I heard someone say, *"beelzebub,"* and I wasn't aware at the time who that was, but I now know it means devil. It didn't frighten me at the time, but mom and dad changed bedrooms with me. After I moved to the new room I started to hear someone breathing on a pillow by my head; maybe even snoring at times. If I moved my bed, it would get quiet for awhile. But sooner or later it would start again. So I became the bed-sharer of a spirit trying to bring fear to me.

We prayed over the house and had other people pray and everything we could do, we did but the house would always return the same even if it stopped for awhile. So one night my dad called from work and said he had movers coming the next day in the morning for us to pack. So we packed and left. We left behind memories good as well as bad.

MY AUNT'S FARM

CHAPTER THREE

My aunt had a farm and a crow that had babies. Those babies had epilepsy and she gave us one. They would fall out of the trees in a seizure. Well, our crow fell into seizures and would fall over. Then he'd get up shake himself and go on. He would put his throat down a certain way and talk. He said several things. He would play and interact with us. He was very sweet. My dad would go by the bait store and buy him worms. One morning, he woke up, had a seizure and died. About two months after he died, I started having seizures until my dad took me to a revival service and had me prayed over and I never took on another seizure. The crow died and I was delivered from seizures before we moved.

Getting back to moving day, we moved into a new house that had never been lived in before. No more noises or strange appearances again. We let the old house go back to the loan company. They sold it, and the people lived in it for a small amount of time but then moved out after about six months. The loan company called mom and dad trying to get them to take it back. They said the people who lived there told them they never had so much bad luck as when they were in that home and that they had no rest there. They heard noises and saw things and they just couldn't stay. Dad and mom didn't take it back.

Sometimes demons will get in a dwelling and what they are looking for is a body to possess. They like to scare and place fear as a weapon against happiness and peace. They prey on one's thoughts especially to possess if possible. If you notice when the evil spirit hit my brother and I hard in the hallway, the Lord put it on both our hearts to pray. That's what protected us. They like to cause fear. Perfect love casts out fear, (1 John 4:18).

This perfected love often refers to the concept of experiencing and expressing God's love more fully, both in receiving and giving to others. This process involves growing in and understanding God's love, refreshing it in our interactions and overcoming fear through His love. The feeling that I felt going from my head to my feet, I believed the Lord was protecting me, covering me and calling me to prayer. As my brother and I were praying, we were protected.

We moved to a new house, it felt like we were starting all over after a tragic time in our lives. The battles we had were over. But we were to still fight new battles because we are saved Christians. There's a real battle going on in the spiritual plane. It rages at times just like the old **FAIRVIEW**, sometimes it's quiet.

My dad came home from his job one morning after working the late shift. He was talking to me about someone who had died in a strange way instantly. I don't want to speak here of how he died because I did at one point thinking I could share this with someone else who said she had no fear. But I seemed to cause fear to come on her by revealing this thing. Fear is of the devil and he uses it in different ways. Christians have power over the devil, but so often we doubt and let fear torment us. Well, a little bit after dad's and my conversation that fear hit me. It was so strong, I felt like I was going to die and instantly. It became so severe I felt a dark cloud was hanging over my head day and night. It was demon oppression, I was having my mother pray for me and when she got close enough to touch me, and it would attack her. I saw no help; I was living in severe fear. I went to sleep and I had a dream. I was sitting at a long table, just me on one end and the devil (satan) on the other when I realized who he was, I got up but so did he. I was in conflict with him. He was standing off from me with this thing (like a wand; or like a scepter of light) in his hand pointing it toward me. It had power in it and he would bring it down and fear would come on me from my head down, all over my body. It was kind of like the feeling my brother and I had in the hall but this wasn't feeling, it was indescribable fear, horrible uncontrollable fear. I closed my eyes in the dream and I began to plead the blood of Jesus, when I opened my eyes he was gone and the fear was gone too.

We're soldiers in the battle of the Lord as Christians. If you joined up with Jesus you're in the army and will indeed have times you must fight. Some people just think it means you will have battles like natural trials but you will also have other battles on a spiritual level but Jesus and the joy He brings and His blessings are worth every battle; and we have the promise of heaven and peace and joy forever. My battle (this battle) was over by pleading the blood, it defeated the devil. He had shown me in a dream how to conquer the enemy.

BATTLES WILL BE FOUGHT

CHAPTER FOUR

*M*uch later in life I have crossed paths with several people who are fighting different kinds of fear and it attacks their minds and because of what I have been through, I know and work diligently to help others going through these things also. If you are struggling with fear, depression or something similar just pray to draw close to Jesus and he'll fight the battles for you.

Scriptures like:

Exodus 14:14
"The LORD will fight for you, and you shall hold your peace."

And

Deuteronomy 20:4
*'for the L*ORD *your God is He who goes with you, to fight for you against your enemies, to save you.'*

During spiritual battles we are called to stand firm in faith and trust in God's strength:

Philippians 4:13
I can do all things through Christ who strengthens me.

In some battles the Lord will fight for you and you need only to be silent. Sometimes we need to fight by standing firm, holding our position and seeing the salvation of the Lord on our behalf. Through scripture we are shown:

2 Chronicles 20:17
*You will not need to fight in this battle. Position yourselves, stand still and see the salvation of the L*ORD*, who is with you, O Judah and Jerusalem!' Do not fear or be dismayed; tomorrow go out against them, for the L*ORD *is with you."*

The devil has many weapons to use against God's people but in scripture it says this:

Isaiah 54:17
No weapon formed against you
shall prosper,
And every tongue which rises against you
in judgment
You shall condemn.
This is the heritage of the servants of
the Lord,
And their righteousness is from Me,"
Says the Lord.

Satan may come at you through trouble in finances:

Psalm 34:17
The righteous cry out, and the Lord hears,
And delivers them out of all their troubles.

Sometimes we have to wait patiently for the Lord to move. At times this is hard, but he will move in his timing and in his own way. Don't let yourself question Him. Just learn to lean on him and to trust him knowing his promises are true.

Isaiah 40:31
But those who wait on the Lord
Shall renew their strength;
They shall mount up with wings like eagles,
They shall run and not be weary,
They shall walk and not faint.

And

Luke 10:19
Behold, I give you the authority to trample on serpents and scorpions, and over all the power of the enemy, and nothing shall by any means hurt you.

We are called to resist the devil too. This is another way of fighting our battles.

James 4:7
Therefore submit to God. Resist the devil and he will flee from you.

And

1 John 4:4
You are of God, little children, and have overcome them, because He who is in you is greater than he who is in the world.

Jesus has power over the devil. He will be with us regardless of the battle you're going through, spiritual, deliverance from something, gossip, financial, health wise or whatever it might be, Jesus has power over it. Attacks are more common than you think. Certain doctors think its mental depression and give patients medications to help them when it's a spiritual battle and all these medications do is dope someone up until they're out of the battle.

My mother gave birth to me, and she wasn't doing well. She was in a second floor bedroom and was told to stay off the stairs. My grandmother had checked on her and went back downstairs to get her some food. It was while she was alone she heard a voice, it sounded like it was talking in a barrel. It was saying her name. she kept moving around the room getting away from it until (like me in the hall) came down over her from her head to her feet like speaking in a barrel calling her name. My grandmother was just coming back upstairs and she heard it also. She said it sounded like it was coming from the bottom of my mother's dress tail. This was an attack. My mother knew how to pray and call upon Jesus. She served the Lord most of her life. She told another Christian woman how she was being fought and the woman says he never bothers me. Well, if he's never fighting you maybe you need to take another prayer trip because you could be on the other's side.

Fairview seemed to be a gateway for evil spirits. We could pray it into quiet, but it was a constant battle. We had others to come in and pray; services in the house but it always seemed to worsen the situation after a quiet spell. Jesus came to give us life and life more abundantly.

John 10:10
The thief does not come except to steal, and to kill, and to destroy. I have come that they may have life, and that they may have it more abundantly.

God desires that his children are living a life full of happiness, peace and a genuine friendship with him. This scripture in John 10:10 means to us to have a super abundance of things in life. The devil wants us to stay away from the purpose of God for our lives. He comes to steal, kill and destroy you. Demons are believed to thrive on fear as they instill anxiety, doubt, despair and more fear.

When you come to Jesus, you are free from all that. He wants us to have free will. He wants us to come to him and serve him because we love him. The devil wants control over you. Some demonic figures are described as seeking control over individual situations or even entire societies. They stir up conflict and strife between people groups and even whole nations. Demons seek to possess people, control their thinking, use them for evil, and the ultimate goal is to take souls to hell. Jesus came to save us from hell. Sin became so great that no sacrifice was great enough to save us from hell until God sent his only begotten Son to be a sacrifice for our sins and dying on the cross and resurrection on the third day gave us salvation if we'll accept him, eternal life, and an abundant life here on earth. Jesus bore stripes as he was beaten for our healing. He left us with free will. He loves us so much and your soul needs this.

Your soul needs to be guarded from the devil. When we allow ourselves to put scary things in our minds like really scary movies, ghost hunts, the occult practices, horoscopes, yoga, etc.: it causes us to feed these things into our souls and sometimes the devil uses those things to place fear in us as a wide open door. It's just like you allow yourself to watch things with lust, desire and filth then you will be feeding your soul these things. Your soul needs spiritual food, the word of God to refresh it. But if you feed it the wrong food you're hurting your soul and causing it to be sick just like if you were feeding your body the wrong things until you become sick physically.

I DON'T KNOW WHAT HAPPENED AT FAIRVIEW

CHAPTER FIVE

I don't know what happened at Fairview. There appeared to be blood stains all over the hardwood floors and on the downstairs staircase treads. There was red hair plastered in the walls in places, I believe there was some kind of evil spiritual practices that opened doors to evil. I don't know, but I do know the place was a battleground for Christians. Through the Lord we survived. We tried our hardest to change Fairview and we couldn't. It was time for us to just move on as it was wearing us down, causing fear and constant battles against evil. We loved the house and we fought for several years, we won the battles, but they kept coming. Every time we would think it was over, after a long quiet time, it would start again. It was just time to move on; we had prayed over every wall inside and outside as well as anointed them with oil.

Going to real haunted houses, ghost hunting and such is dangerous, as well as going into maximum security prisons that are haunted. How much more danger can you put yourself into spiritually while you're opening up yourself to evil spirits? These demons are not to be played with; they're after your soul. They hate humans. They want to control you here on earth to take away your own will which is God-given. Finally, they want to send your soul to hell, please heed this warning; don't open yourself up to these spirits.

You may think you're dealing with dead or ghost spirits of people; but they may even take on the form of someone who has died to fool you, but they are not, they are evil spirits; demons after your soul. They may even take on the form of a child, but those spirits are not children. They seek to deceive you and do deceive many. Please don't be fooled by their antics. They are creatures of darkness. They seek evil. Jesus seeks only good for you giving you eternal life. Jesus is the light; he is the light of the world. (John 8:12) he will take the loneliness, anxiety, heartache or whatever is in your life that makes you sad or lonely, or anxious or fearful and make the light shine on your darkness until you feel joy and peace. Happiness, peace and joy only come from God. Yes, you can have joyful days, but the joy and peace I speak of is in the soul.

Many times people see and hear things in places where a murder or some tragic death took place. My dad worked at a chemical plant and they had an accident while he was off on vacation. A man he worked with was burned so severely he passed away. He was at the hospital talking to people under a sheet because of his burns, and then he died. Dad came back from vacation and found out about his death. Dad knew him well, shortly after his death the man was seen on the walk ways around the plant. Some of the men saw this man that died walking on one of them. Some say that because of the violence on the scene was imported to the atmosphere. Well, they say that the sound never leaves the atmosphere. I have a theory that I believe evil spirits were in a person when they died, now they linger to possess someone else. I also think that an evil spirit entices someone to murder another so they can possess another. They repeat the scene over and over getting joy out of scaring others drawing them into fear themselves.

There are good spirits, such as angels, unlike the evil ones, they are operating in good directed by God. They are more powerful and appear to us sometimes; when my dad's brother's baby passed away, this was years ago and the neighbors would set up all night with the bodies. They had the baby laid out in my uncle's house. It was hot outside in the middle of summer. They didn't have air conditioning like today. They were living in a small country town, so they opened the windows and the doors. Late that night while they sat up with the baby, a light came in the room by the door. It hovered over the baby then went out the window. They thought it was an angel coming for the baby's soul. I believe this also, it didn't come as anything fearful, but as a ball of light.

Angels are sent to help and protect us. I believe we all have a guardian angel from the time we're born. When I was about eight years of age, my cousins and I were swinging on a grapevine across a high embankment. I had swung several times along with everyone else, but then I was in line and felt really strong to get out of line and not swing that time. One of my cousins took my place and the grapevine broke, hurting her back badly. It could have been me, it would have hurt me worse, maybe killed me, I don't know. She asked me if I knew the vine was going to break. I didn't know why, I just felt not to swing. Angels are sent to help us, but we still have free will. We have to listen when a warning is coming to us. Some won't even listen to the Lord much less an angel. I went to Bible College with a girl who told me she had a dream that she was walking down a road and Jesus was talking to her, but she was ignoring him. She asked me what does that mean? I said I think it means exactly what it was. He's trying to talk to you, but you're not listening.

MY OIL PAINTINGS

CHAPTER SIX

The oil painting I spoke about at the beginning of the book, I painted it when I first started painting. I wasn't really good at it then, but you can see what Fairview looked like. When you look at a place on the outside, you cannot imagine what's on the inside.

I painted oil paintings for years. I paint landscapes and people. I started painting in my thirties. I can't tell you how many I've done over the years. I belonged to several art guilds in that time. I started painting when I was teaching the lower grades in a Christian School, drawing and painting the small children.

I just finished a new painting of the Holy Dove; our Pastor has put it up in our church. The highest I have ever sold a painting for is

$275.00. The Lord has blessed me with this talent. I can only paint when the talent comes, I can't paint on my own. I told the Lord one time to send the painter; I'm sure he laughed at me and said,

"You are the painter."

I painted Fairview many years ago when I first started painting. It isn't my best work but it was a heart-felt painting. I have taken several painting classes. One teacher I had taught me water colors. I lived in Aurora, Indiana at the time and took her class after my mother passed and it helped me get over it. Yes, it surely did. My mom and dad owned the house in Aurora at the time I painted a water color of the house in a Christmas setting. It helped me a lot and she inspired me to keep painting.

My husband and I were looking for a house and we found this beautiful house. It was a two-story house. We really loved it and it was like Fairview. It had a welcoming atmosphere. We hadn't seen the inside of it, but we were to see it the next day. That night I dreamed we had bought a house and were getting ready to go to bed. I saw the living room, family room, dining room, kitchen, the upstairs hall and the bedrooms and I was going downstairs to check the door to make sure it was locked. When I got to the bottom of the stairs I saw a bright light coming out of the rooms going down the hallway. The next day we went to see the house and I knew each room because of my dream. I had seen it all. I was describing the rooms before I got into them. The realtor said, *"Oh you've been in the house before?"*

I said, *"No,"* and told him of my dream. We would have bought the house but after that dream, we would not. The realtor forgot some papers in the house, but wouldn't go back inside alone, but asked my husband to go back with him. This was a form of the light, but I don't believe this light was any angel. Sometimes evil will appear as an angel of light when it is really the opposite. Scripture tells us this:

2 Corinthians 11:14
*And no wonder! For Satan himself transforms himself into an **angel of light**.*

My grandpa and grandma bought a country home and it was very much like Fairview. It wasn't a peaceful home. The inside of the house was good but outside they could see a woman walking and sometimes running. My dad was small at the time, and he and his brother were playing outside when grandpa and grandma were not home. Dad was from a large family, he was the youngest which was number seven. The neighbors would bring babies to him that had thrush and have him blow in their mouth because of a fable that the seventh son would have the gift of healing. As he grew up God indeed gave him the gift of healing through the Holy Spirit. Let's get back to he and his brother playing. They were fussing, so dad said,

"I wish I had someone to play with."

He and his brother saw that woman coming, she was almost running. Dad's brother ran and locked the door from the inside, locking my dad outside. Dad said he was so scared. He was beating on the door, trying to get his brother to open up but he wouldn't. The woman came up to the porch of the house and left dad alone. She just kept going around to the back of the house. What she was, I don't know, but she brought a lot of fear to these two little boys. Fear is from the devil, it isn't anything good. The first thing in the Bible, when angels appeared to humans, they would say, *'fear not.'*

The area they lived in was a field, where a feud was fought. People saw a lot of things there because of the hate and the murders that were done. One side of the field had a cemetery real close on the hillside. Dad and Mom built a house down from it before my brother and I were ever born. The church people would walk to services there and back past their house and one night they heard people talking and laughing and thought it was the church people coming back. But they looked there, and there wasn't anyone there.

My grandpa started going to church one night walking alone. The church people usually males and females walk together. He saw a woman in the distance walking toward the church. He called out and hurried up to join her, but when he got closer, she had no head. It was vanishing, and soon her whole body disappeared. I believe she may have been a victim in that field, and some demons enjoying their victory. Demons are evil death and destruction and fear are their happiness, and they love to cause fear.

As Christians we don't have to fear those things. The Lord protects His children. My grandpa was safe, he was a Baptist Minister.

Why are these things happening? We are in a spiritual war between good and evil. In a battle for souls, this is not a play thing to go ghost hunting or running to haunted houses.

You might as well say I'm going to a demon infested house, maybe I'll take one home with me. Many people have just by going and opening themselves up to them. One of my sons got a spirit in his house. My husband and I went to pray over his house, anointing it with oil to get out. The Spirit of the Lord came and we felt the most wonderful victory.

When it was gone, I began to sing and rejoice. I was a little surprised it went so easy. We went home a few days after that. I was in the bedroom and I heard something calling my name. I thought at first I had imagined it, I'm a little hard of hearing. I kept hearing something, and then it screamed my name right in my face. I was so startled, I screamed. My husband came into the room. I felt it, and we prayed it out. That spirit we thought was so easy to go out at my son's, well we brought it home in our car and came home with us and causing fear.

Dad had to drive by a cemetery on his way home from work one night. He felt someone in the car with him a short distance, and then it left. When a Christian dies, the Bible says to be absent from the body is to be present with the Lord. (2 Corinthians 5:8) the Lord's children are not wandering around here on earth, scaring people. So who are these beings? Demons are some of those who left the body when someone who died is simply looking for another home. They must have a host to live in.

FAITH OVER FEAR

CHAPTER SEVEN

𝓐 good Christian woman was in a tent revival of A.A. Allen and he was casting out demons up in front of the tent. She was in the back of the tent, not really paying attention. Reverend Allen told everyone before he cast a demon out to get their minds on the Lord and pray. Well, she kept talking, the demons came out, but they couldn't enter her being a Christian. But they ran into her, knocked her down and broke her hip. When someone is casting out demons, pay attention and get your mind in God. Demons are real, but so is God's power and his power is so much stronger than anything the devil offers.

FAITH OVER FEAR

Psalm 91

Safety of Abiding in the Presence of God

*1 He who dwells in the secret place of the
Most High
Shall abide under the shadow of
the Almighty.*

*2 I will say of the L*ORD*, "He is my refuge
and my fortress;
My God, in Him I will trust."*

*3 Surely He shall deliver you from the snare
of the fowler
And from the perilous pestilence.*

*4 He shall cover you with His feathers,
And under His wings you shall take refuge;
His truth shall be your shield and buckler.*

*5 You shall not be afraid of the terror
by night,
Nor of the arrow that flies by day,*

*6 Nor of the pestilence that walks
in darkness,
Nor of the destruction that lays waste
at noonday.*

*7 A thousand may fall at your side,
And ten thousand at your right hand;
But it shall not come near you.*

*8 Only with your eyes shall you look,
And see the reward of the wicked.*

*9 Because you have made the L<small>ORD</small>, who
is my refuge,
Even the Most High, your dwelling place,*

*10 No evil shall befall you,
Nor shall any plague come near
your dwelling;*

*11 For He shall give His angels charge
over you,
To keep you in all your ways.*

*12 In their hands they shall bear you up,
Lest you dash your foot against a stone.*

*13 You shall tread upon the lion and
the cobra,
The young lion and the serpent you shall
trample underfoot.*

*14 "Because he has set his love upon Me,
therefore I will deliver him;
I will set him on high, because he has known
My name.*

*15 He shall call upon Me, and I will answer him;
I will be with him in trouble;
I will deliver him and honor him.*

*16 With long life I will satisfy him,
And show him My salvation."*

I have placed this complete chapter in this writing because it is important you read it and meditate on it. Fear can cause confusion, anxiety, torment, and depression. Faith will cause love, joy and peace.

When you abide in the secret place, you are under God's protection. If you don't have a secret place to talk to God, you need to find one; a place where you talk to God and listen while he talks to you. It's a special prayer corner or closet.

God sends his angels to protect you. My dad stepped off a curb onto a busy highway, and two strong men came on each side of him and pulled him back off of the highway just as a car was coming fast. Then dad looked around for the men, but they were gone. He knew it had to have been angels.

Psalm 34:7
The angel of the L<small>ORD</small> *encamps all around those who fear Him,*
And delivers them.

DEMON MANIFESTATION

When out of a body demons manifest themselves in different ways. In Fairview they were manifesting by apparitions, hearing, talking, knocking, and even touching. The purpose of showing themselves in these manors, it was to frighten. They desire to possess and it usually starts with fear unless one is yielding to sin.

Yielding to temptation can cause possession if it is constant, example: one starts lying, then they keep telling one lie after another until they finally get so they can't talk without lying. A lying demon can take control so that a person has no more control over lying. This is the same as cursing. One begins cursing and they get so they can't talk without cursing. A minister's son began cursing away from his home, he kept cursing until he couldn't talk without cursing. He had to watch himself around his father because he was so out of control with his tongue.

Lust, adultery, and fornication: these things start out by doing the sins of them. If it is cultivated and continued, it will get ahold of you and maybe even destroy your life or get possessed. Don't feed your soul evil things. Watching filthy movies for example can cause a lustful spirit to get ahold of you, also stealing; murder, adultery, etc. are things we don't need to feed our souls. Christians will be condemned.

Christians will be condemned when they dabble in sin. Listen to the Holy Spirit's voice leading you away from dangers to your soul. Protect your inner man by being careful in what you see and hear. Prayer is a weapon against evil; prayer is your door to faith.

Romans 10:17
So then faith comes by hearing, and hearing by the word of God.

This scripture verse emphasizes that true faith is a result of actively listening to and engaging with the message of Christ as presented here and proclaimed by Bible believers. It highlights the importance of preaching, teaching and sharing the gospel message to foster faith. This also indicates faith is not a natural human ability, but rather a response to hearing the word of Christ.

Hebrews 12:2
looking unto Jesus, the author and finisher of our faith, who for the joy that was set before Him endured the cross, despising the shame, and has sat down at the right hand of the throne of God.

1. Perfect Peace – when Jesus remains our focus, your heart is filled with perfect peace.

2. True Unity – when Jesus remains your focus, you'll experience true unity with other believers.

3. Spiritual Stability – when Jesus remains your focus, you feel an overwhelming stability in your life.

4. Effectiveness – when you keep Jesus close to you, his Spirit will be effective and sure.

1 John 4:18
There is no fear in love;
but perfect love casts out fear, because fear
involves torment. But he who fears has not
been made perfect in love.

If we grow closer to Jesus, our love grows stronger, his love is manifested in us, and our faith grows so we can overcome fear or withstand evil.

John 16:33
"These things I have spoken to you, that in Me you may have peace. In the world you will have tribulation; but be of good cheer, I have overcome the world."

As Christians through prayers we are kept safe from any possession that could have taken place when demons existed at Fairview. Jesus sends his holy angels to protect us and the Holy Spirit to guide us in the ways to overcome evil.

I believe the feelings my brother and I had in the upstairs hallway at Fairview were from the Lord, calling us to prayer to protect us, maybe from possession as we were both angry, quarreling and in doing so, leaving ourselves open for the enemy to attack. The feelings were awful, but the devil doesn't call you to prayer.

There's a spiritual world all around us, the war of good and evil. The battle is for souls. The devil seeks to gain as many souls as he can to take them to hell. He hates the humans whom God created in his own image. The Lord wants us all to be saved from hell and seeks to bless us and to prosper us here on earth. He loved us so much, he died on the cross and rose again the third day to bring salvation to us.

HAUNTED HOUSES

CHAPTER EIGHT

People run, especially on Halloween to haunted houses. What they don't realize they are chasing demons. It's opening themselves up to them. They sometimes go home with these people, causing them fear, tormenting them, and the ultimate goal is to possess them. Playing with your children's lives by giving them candy or letting them dress up in outfits is one thing, but chasing real spirits is dangerous spiritually.

When my sons were teenagers, they wanted to go to a haunted house. I didn't mind them playing on Halloween, a fake fun hayride or costumes, but I felt really bad about them going to a haunted house, especially. I didn't know why at the time, but I really felt it strong not to let them go there. One of my sons said that was the way the teachers felt also. I asked why? It seems this house is where a dentist and his family were murdered, and then they made a haunted house of it. The murderer had never been caught. Someone thought this was a good idea for Halloween. After this, they tried to sell the house, but no one would buy it. They tried to give the house away, to have it moved, but no one took it. So the city had the house torn down. Well, needless to say we did not go to this house on Halloween. This house could have had murder demons in it, since the murderer had not been caught. He could have been going through this also, demon possessed.

Dad, mom, my husband and I, would pray over people who were possessed and over houses that had demons in them, and saw them delivered. Fairview was different, our prayers would protect us and stop the activity for awhile, but it would always return. Why? I can't really say, we had to finally leave. Sometimes demon activity has been practiced in a house and opens doorways, such as satan worshippers. God has power over the devil, but just like he doesn't heal everyone, every place is not delivered. We could have seen so much and been tormented and scared so much, it may have hindered our faith. It was a very hard trial of faith.

One needs to be careful of the items you bring into your home also. Sometimes spirits attach themselves to items. My husband and I went to a garage sale, years ago, and we bought a beautiful old antique dresser, with metal handles. I was staying at my dad's house at the time taking care of him and I refinished the dresser on his patio. I then put it in storage until I was ready to go home. When I got home, I took it out of storage and put it in my bedroom. I started to hear the metal handles clicking up and down all through the house. I checked and saw the handles moving up and down on their own. I thought at first it was something directing me to check drawers out. There was nothing in the drawers. It continued and brought about fear. My husband and I prayed over the dresser, anointing it with oil, and asked the Lord to move whatever it was, out of our house and we never heard the noises again.

Years after Fairview, my mom and dad moved into a small town in Aurora, Indiana, where part of the Civil War was fought. They moved into a large house that used to be a doctor's office. It was a peaceful place by the river. The riverboats would go up and down the Ohio River. They were beautiful. The town was plagued with spirits from the Civil War. There were very few of the homes that escaped them. My mom and dad prayed constantly in their home and nothing came in the main house. They would hear walking across the floor of the attic, except there was no floor in the attic. They never came into the house, as long as mom and dad still lived there. They both passed away and my husband and I were at the house cleaning things out, and I had been vacuuming downstairs and then I went upstairs. The vacuum was still downstairs and my husband went to the store. I was alone in the house and the vacuum came on by itself downstairs. I thought something was trying to make me think my dad was still there. He had passed away after my mother. I would never believe such a thing. Dad and mom were both ministers and I know they both were with Jesus, I rebuked it.

One of the neighbors came over and asked if she could take pictures inside the house as her home across the street had spirits in it. She wanted to see if she could get anything on camera. I allowed her to do it; she got streaks of light in the pictures. I knew that the prayer and lives that mom and dad had lived, kept the evil out, as long as they lived. A few years before my mother was given a prophecy that something would attack the neighborhood, but would not come into their dwelling. I believe the prophecy was about spirits of evil around them, but not where they dwelt.

PRAYER IS A WEAPON

CHAPTER NINE

Prayer is a weapon against evil. The word of God, the Bible, are our weapons against evil; here in scripture it says this:

2 Corinthians 10:4-6
4 For the weapons of our warfare are not carnal but mighty in God for pulling down strongholds,

5 casting down arguments and every high thing that exalts itself against the knowledge of God, bringing every thought into captivity to the obedience of Christ,

6 and being ready to punish all disobedience when your obedience is fulfilled.

The disciples thought Jesus was a spirit when He came walking on the water to them:

Matthew 14:22-23
Jesus Walks on the Sea

22 And straightway Jesus constrained his disciples to get into a ship, and to go before him unto the other side, while he sent the multitudes away.

23 And when he had sent the multitudes away, he went up into a mountain apart to pray: and when the evening was come, he was there alone.

24 But the ship was now in the midst of the sea, tossed with waves: for the wind was contrary.

25 And in the fourth watch of the night Jesus went unto them, walking on the sea.

26 And when the disciples saw him walking on the sea, they were troubled, saying, It is a spirit; and they cried out for fear.

27 But straightway Jesus spake unto them, saying, Be of good cheer; it is I; be not afraid.

So there must have been spirits even then, and we have the Holy Spirit. (Luke 24) Jesus showed the disciples because they were terrified again, that he was a ghost, then showing them his physical body. He had them touch him and see for a ghost does not have flesh and bones as he did, then they could see. He even ate a piece of fish in their presence. Jesus resurrected his body as well as his spirit. He was transformed into a glorified body, it shows how we will be transformed one day.

We don't have to walk or live in fear of these things like spirits or demons. Christ has power over them, and he gave us that power too. (Luke 10:19) But we do need to be informed and have a walk with the Lord to overcome them. I've overcome fear in many situations, but always with assistance from the Lord.

A lot of people don't believe these things I've told you in this book, but some people don't believe there are demons or angels either. That doesn't make them any less real. The war rages on whether they believe it or not. It's a day when people need to open up their eyes to the spiritual warfare that's going on. How can you defend yourself from an attack if you don't believe its happening? We need to do as the Bible tells us to put on the whole armor of God:

Ephesians 6:11-20
11 Put on the whole armor of God, that you may be able to stand against the wiles of the devil.

12 For we do not wrestle against flesh and blood, but against principalities, against powers, against the rulers of the darkness of this age, against spiritual hosts of wickedness in the heavenly places.

13 Therefore take up the whole armor of God, that you may be able to withstand in the evil day, and having done all, to stand.

14 Stand therefore, having girded your waist with truth, having put on the breastplate of righteousness,

15 and having shod your feet with the preparation of the gospel of peace;

16 above all, taking the shield of faith with which you will be able to quench all the fiery darts of the wicked one.

17 And take the helmet of salvation, and the sword of the Spirit, which is the word of God;

18 praying always with all prayer and supplication in the Spirit, being watchful to this end with all perseverance and supplication for all the saints—

19 and for me, that utterance may be given to me, that I may open my mouth boldly to make known the mystery of the gospel,

20 for which I am an ambassador in chains; that in it I may speak boldly, as I ought to speak.

If you choose to believe in human spirits, I cannot disapprove it except for in Christians. (2 Corinthians 5:8) To be absent from the body is to be present with the Lord. Stephen who was stoned in the Bible, a man of faith was a Christian martyr. As he died, he saw the heavens open and saw the glory of God, Jesus standing on the right hand of God, the Father. (Acts 6-7) Our Lord has prepared a place for our souls. He loves and takes care of his children.

Demons are extremely persistent if you drive one out, it will still seek to force its way back in again. See scripture as Jesus speaks:

Matthew 12:43-45
An Unclean Spirit Returns

43 "When an unclean spirit goes out of a man, he goes through dry places, seeking rest, and finds none.

44 Then he says, 'I will return to my house from which I came.' And when he comes, he finds it empty, swept, and put in order.

45 Then he goes and takes with him seven other spirits more wicked than himself, and they enter and dwell there; and the last state of that man is worse than the first. So shall it also be with this wicked generation."

Christians don't have to fear possession because in order to be possessed, they would have to go completely away from the Lord, no man can serve two masters. (Matthew 6:24) But oppression can take place, tormenting the believer to distraction. One must be led by the Holy Spirit and anointed to cast out demons. See scripture here:

Acts 19:14-16
14 Also there were seven sons of Sceva, a Jewish chief priest, who did so.

15 And the evil spirit answered and said, "Jesus I know, and Paul I know; but who are you?"

16 Then the man in whom the evil spirit was leaped on them, overpowered them, and prevailed against them, so that they fled out of that house naked and wounded.

Be aware that demons are evil spirits who will challenge you. The sons of Skeva in these scripture verses of the Book of Acts, chapter nineteen shows us to beware, and these demonic forces prevailed against them. So they fled out of the house naked and wounded. Demon entities recognize the authority of Jesus and Paul who followed him, but they questioned the sons of Skeva and attacked them, humiliating them. The demon reacts to the name of Paul because it knows Paul has the power of Jesus. It reacts to the name of Jesus because it knows Jesus is the Son of God. In scripture:

Mark 1:24
saying, "Let us alone! What have we to do with You, Jesus of Nazareth? Did You come to destroy us? I know who You are—the Holy One of God!"

There was a man in the synagogue with an unclean spirit, and he cried out saying, *"Let us alone!"* You've read the rest of the scripture acknowledging that He is the Holy One of God. (Mark 3:11) When unclean spirits saw Jesus they fell down before him, and cried, saying thou are the Son of God. They know who Jesus is and they bow. The scribes from Jerusalem said Jesus was casting out devils by Beelzebub, the prince of devils and that he had been beguiled. (Matthew 12:24-27)

And

Matthew 10:25
It is enough for a disciple that he be like his teacher, and a servant like his master. If they have called the master of the house Beelzebub, how much more will they call those of his household!

Jesus has the power to cast out demons by the Holy Spirit that empowers all that love him.

People foolishly dabble in the things of the occult. They let children play with things like ouija boards, séances, horoscopes and devils. They look to satan worship to entertain with witchcraft. Some are saying these are good witches; wicca and such nonsense. To worship the devil is not good; it's pure evil. The devil doesn't come to people as evil. If he did, they couldn't be deceived. It's a lot easier to get into satanic things than it is to get out of them; satan hangs on for dear life. (your life) Dope starts out as fun, a good feeling until you can't do without it. Alcohol is the same, many drink for pleasure until someone becomes an alcoholic. Our Lord has power over all evil, but we must denounce evil and come to him and repent of these sins committed and give their hearts to Jesus who is Lord. Whom the Son sets free is free indeed. (John 8:36)

SUPERSTITION

CHAPTER TEN

𝓐 lot of superstitions open up doors which cause oppression and fear. Most superstitions are based on fear. Such as chain letters, if you don't write another letter and send it to someone else something awful will happen to you. There is another saying: 'if you step on a crack, you'll break your mother's back; or if you spill salt, you must throw some over your shoulder or you will die. If you notice all of these and many more out there are fear-based trying to control you. Fear is attached to each one of them as a means of control. Fear is from the devil; don't yield to his control, and not even in the small things. If he gets control over the small things, he will try to control you over larger things. See scripture that gives us wisdom:

Ecclesiastes 9:5-6
5 For the living know that they will die;
But the dead know nothing,
And they have no more reward,
For the memory of them is forgotten.

6 Also their love, their hatred, and their envy have now perished;
Nevermore will they have a share
In anything done under the sun.

These scriptures are speaking about in this world, not in the after life. Now, they have no part in this world after death, (the human spirits) then who are the spirits we see here? They are demonic because the saints of God are to be absent from the body and present with the Lord. We don't hang around to bother others. See scripture:

Deuteronomy 18:10-12
10 There shall not be found among you anyone who makes his son or his daughter pass through the fire, or one who practices witchcraft, or a soothsayer, or one who interprets omens, or a sorcerer,

11 or one who conjures spells, or a medium, or a spiritist, or one who calls up the dead.

*12 For all who do these things are an abomination to the L*ORD*, and because of these abominations the L*ORD *your God drives them out from before you.*

This teaches us not to make contact with the dead. It is called *necromancy*. There's another scripture that speaks of it as King Saul sought a witch to speak to the passed on Prophet Samuel: read this with me:

1 Samuel 28:6-17
*6 And when Saul inquired of the L*ORD*, the L*ORD *did not answer him, either by dreams or by Urim or by the prophets.*

7 Then Saul said to his servants, "Find me a woman who is a medium, that I may go to her and inquire of her."
And his servants said to him, "In fact, there is a woman who is a medium at En Dor."

8 So Saul disguised himself and put on other clothes, and he went, and two men with him; and they came to the woman by night. And he said, "Please conduct a séance for me, and bring up for me the one I shall name to you."

9 Then the woman said to him, "Look, you know what Saul has done, how he has cut off the mediums and the spiritists from the land. Why then do you lay a snare for my life, to cause me to die?"

*10 And Saul swore to her by the L*ORD*, saying, "As the L*ORD *lives, no punishment shall come upon you for this thing."*

11 Then the woman said, "Whom shall I bring up for you?"
And he said, "Bring up Samuel for me."

12 When the woman saw Samuel, she cried out with a loud voice. And the woman spoke to Saul, saying, "Why have you deceived me? For you are Saul!"

13 And the king said to her, "Do not be afraid. What did you see?"
And the woman said to Saul, "I saw a spirit ascending out of the earth."

14 So he said to her, "What is his form?" And she said, "An old man is coming up, and he is covered with a mantle." And Saul perceived that it was Samuel, and he stooped with his face to the ground and bowed down.

15 Now Samuel said to Saul, "Why have you disturbed me by bringing me up?" And Saul answered, "I am deeply distressed; for the Philistines make war against me, and God has departed from me and does not answer me anymore, neither by prophets nor by dreams. Therefore I have called you, that you may reveal to me what I should do."

16 Then Samuel said: "So why do you ask me, seeing the LORD has departed from you and has become your enemy?

17 And the LORD has done for Himself as He spoke by me. For the LORD has torn the kingdom out of your hand and given it to your neighbor, David.

This woman Saul sought is from the league of the devil. She had what they call '*a familiar spirit*' or simply a demon by which she was doing this evil thing. Same thing happens today.

People run to a fortune teller or card reader or physic, they have several names, to have their future told. The devil has abilities of fortunetelling the future. God knows the future. When one goes to these devious demons that are connected to evil, they open themselves up to the devil. Now you are in his lair. There are some churches that these spiritualists go to, and people go for the so-called readings to have their future told.

Don't run from place to place seeking answers about your future. Turn to the Lord Jesus Christ. He knows what the future holds and will give you peace to put your future in his hands. (Jeremiah 29:11) He will bless you and guide you by the Holy Spirit. Your blessings will be beyond your wildest dreams. (Ephesians 3:20) He wants to prosper us, and be in health, even as our souls prosper. (3 John 2)

Some of the memories I have of Fairview are good memories, they are playful times and family. My family is all gone to be with the Lord now, but some of those memories at Fairview were so hard to go back over. I can still remember exactly how it felt when that feeling came from my head to my feet in the hallway upstairs. I've gone back in my mind over these things, even though it was years ago to tell you about and warn you that the spirits are not to be played with. I urge you to turn to the Lord, repent of your sins, and let Jesus cover you with his protection. In Jesus we do not have to be afraid because there is no fear in love.

1 John 4:18
There is no fear in love; but perfect love casts out fear, because fear involves torment. But he who fears has not been made perfect in love.

Jesus loved us first. When we come close to our Lord, all fear vanishes away because of his great love. It covers us so completely:

2 Timothy 1:7
For God has not given us a spirit of fear, but of power and of love and of a sound mind.

The devil seeks to destroy you. He is the enemy. He seeks to control your mind. When we turn our lives and souls over to God, he leaves us self will. He doesn't seek to control you. He wants you to serve him out of love for him because he loves us so much. The Lord guides us in the ways he would have us to go. He leads us in the ways of joy and blessings. He speaks to us in so many ways, prophecy through his word, and in our hearts and minds. If you seek an answer, don't run from place to place seeking a word from the Lord, but go directly to him and he will send the answer to you. He loves you and wants you to come directly to him.

I pray this book opens your eyes to the dangers of evil and the warfare that's going on spiritually, but most of all those who turn for fear or deliverance. Our blessed Savior is the conqueror of all evil. The King of kings, the Lord of lords is our Master and Savior Jesus Christ.

*** Publisher's Note: Sharon Taylor King had a car accident with a deer on the night of Sunday, 11/30/2025 after leaving church. Because of this trauma she was removed from the scene by ambulance as it resulted in a heart attack. Before leaving the scene she was outside the car and as she looked up from the road, she saw the people of the church like angels standing all around her praying for her, and singing Amazing Grace, so lovingly. She is now safely recovering and has been in contact with us to go forth with the book. Please pray for her. We want you to know the battle is real but God saved her for such a time as this.

AUTHOR'S BOOK SHELF

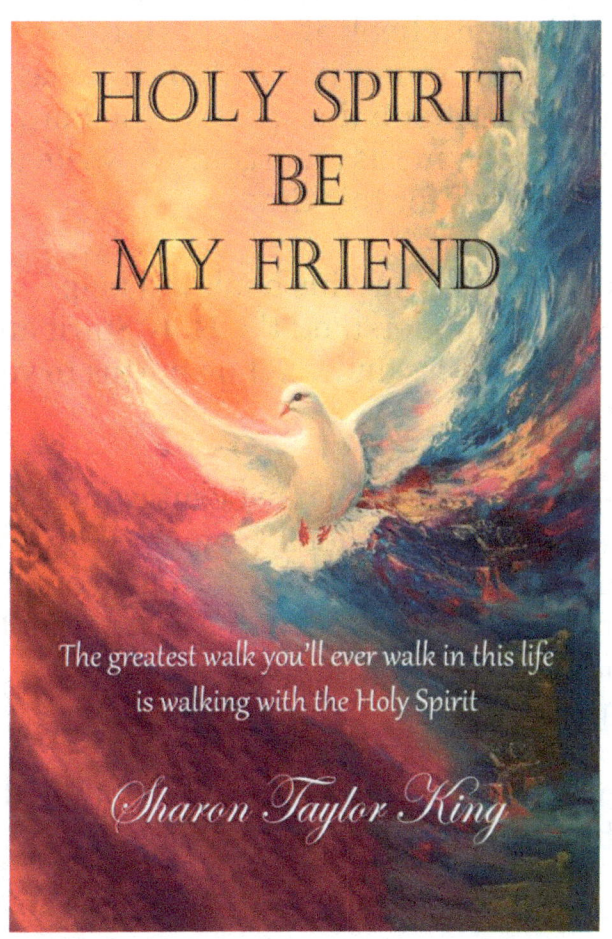

Holy Spirit Be My Friend Paperback –

by Sharon Taylor King (Author)

The greatest walk you'll ever walk in this life is walking with the Holy Spirit.

Many years ago it was prophesied to me that I would write a book about the Holy Spirit. Like as many things in our Bible that has come about after a time passed, the Lord has pressed upon me as an urgency to write it at this time, and for this time.

It is my prayer that this book will help someone to understand the Holy Spirit and realize who he is and what he means to you and I.

The Holy Spirit is the most gentle, most beautiful, most precious, loving person on earth. His touch lifts every burden, comforts every broken heart, brings peace to troubled minds and gives us happiness and joy unspeakable.

There is no power greater on earth than that of the Holy Spirit.

Amazon: Paperback $11.95 Kindle $4.99

AUTHOR'S PICTURES

Fairview Avenue

Sister Sharon Taylor King

Sharon's Father
Hughie E. Taylor

Sharon's Mother
June King Taylor

Sharon's Brother
Ronald E. Taylor

Made in the USA
Coppell, TX
30 December 2025

67505427R00046